Filipino Heritage
Celebrating Diversity in My Classroom

By Tamra B. Orr

21st Century
Junior Library

CHERRY LAKE Publishing

Published in the United States of America by
Cherry Lake Publishing
Ann Arbor, Michigan
www.cherrylakepublishing.com

Reading Adviser: Marla Conn MS, Ed., Literacy specialist, Read-Ability, Inc.

Photo Credits: © asiastock / Shutterstock Images, cover; © Alyona Naive Angel / Shutterstock Images, 4; © Anna ART / Shutterstock Images, 6; © View Apart / Shutterstock Images, 8; © Tony Magdaraog / Shutterstock Images, 10, 12; © ARTRAN / Shutterstock Images, 14; © Maria Maarbes / Shutterstock Images, 16; © Akhenaton Images / Shutterstock Images, 18; © Ekaterina Pokrovsky / Shutterstock Images, 20

Library of Congress Cataloging-in-Publication Data
Name: Orr, Tamra, author.
Title: Filipino heritage / by Tamra B. Orr.
Description: Ann Arbor : Cherry Lake Publishing, 2018. | Series: Celebrating diversity in my classroom | Includes bibliographical references and index. | Audience: Grade K to 3.
Identifiers: LCCN 2017035945 | ISBN 9781534107366 (hardcover) | ISBN 9781534109346 (pdf) | ISBN 9781534108356 (pbk.) | ISBN 9781534120334 (hosted ebook)
Subjects: LCSH: Philippines—Juvenile literature.
Classification: LCC DS655 .O77 2018 | DDC 959.9—dc23
LC record available at https://lccn.loc.gov/2017035945

Cherry Lake Publishing would like to acknowledge the work of The Partnership for 21st Century Skills.
Please visit *www.p21.org* for more information.

Printed in the United States of America
Corporate Graphics

CONTENTS

Some of the rice fields in the Philippines are more than 2,000 years old.

Fabulous Philippines

The Philippines is an **archipelago** scattered across the water. There are more than 7,000 of these islands. But only 2,000 have people living on them.

Most of the people in the Philippines live on one of the two biggest islands. Luzon, in the north, or Mindanao in the south.

Many people from the Philippines have **emigrated** to countries all over the world. There are about 2 million **immigrants** from the Philippines in the United States! What is their home country like?

"*Magandang umaga*" means "good morning!" in Filipino.

Magandang araw!

Do you know how to speak **Filipino**? You will soon! *"Magandang araw!"* means "Beautiful day!" It is a common way the Filipinos greet each other. Other greetings are *"Magandang umaga"* for "Good morning" and *"Magandang gabi"* for "Good night."

Tagalog is the original language on the main islands. But more people speak English than they do Tagalog. People speak

Most students in the Philippines can speak at least two languages.

English in schools, restaurants, hotels, and government offices! People also speak "Taglish." This is a combination of the two languages. *"Gets mo?"* means "Do you understand?" *"Relax ka lang"* means "Take it easy!"

More than 175 languages are spoken across the islands. Each one is a little different than the next. Some include Spanish words since the islands once belonged to Spain.

Millions of people follow the parade during the
Feast of the Black Nazarene.

Religious Traditions

There are millions of Roman Catholics in the Philippines. Every January, they join together to celebrate the Feast of the Black **Nazarene**. It takes place in Manila. People take off their shoes. Then they get in line behind a huge black statue of Jesus Christ. They follow as the statue is slowly carried through the city. They hope to be able to touch the statue. They believe that the statue has healing powers.

The Aliwan Festival celebrates the many different cultural traditions of the Philippines.

Most of the countries in nearby Asia follow religions such as Buddhism or Islam. The Philippines is mainly Catholic, especially on the larger islands. Many people blend their beliefs with an old religion called **animism**. This belief states that all living things have spirits, including trees and plants.

Think!

Filipinos love basketball! Baskets are put up almost everywhere. Local teams are always forming and playing across the islands. Filipinos also love boxing. An interesting thing happens when their favorite boxers have a match. There is almost no crime in the city! Why do you think that happens?

Eating on banana leaves is part of *kamayan* style dining.

Finger Foods and Banana Leaves

Don't like washing dishes? You might like eating the way many Filipinos do. The table is covered in big, green banana leaves. There are no plates. The food is placed directly on the leaves. And people don't eat with forks, knives, and spoons. They use something much simpler. They pick up meat, vegetables, and desserts with their fingers. Soup is served in bowls but not with spoons. It is sipped!

Markets in the Philippines serve lots of delicious food.

Some countries like salty or sweet foods. But Filipinos love sour flavors. They use a lot of vinegar in cooking. *Camaro* is popular in some areas. This is field crickets cooked in soy sauce, vinegar, and sugar. *Adobo* is the national dish. It is a dark stew made out of chicken or pork. It has soy sauce, vinegar, garlic, pepper, and coconut milk added. Almost everything is served with rice on the side. And since Filipinos are surrounded by oceans, fish is always a popular dish!

Filipinos send more text messages than the United States
and Europe combined!

From Texting Capital to Traffic Jams

Quick! What country do you think sends the most text messages every day? Most people would guess the United States. But the Philippines is known as the "texting capital of the world." Filipinos send out 400 million text messages a day! That adds up to 146 *billion* a year!

Cities in the Philippines are crowded. Getting around in some of them can be an

Parol are made from bamboo and usually in the shape of a star.

adventure. Many Filipinos rely on *jeepneys*. These taxi-like vehicles are made out of jeeps. They have been made longer and can hold as many as 18 people. If you need a ride, get ready to run! The jeepneys do not stop for passengers. Instead, you run and jump on. You pass your money to the driver. And you jump off when you get to where you are going.

Look!

No one does Christmas bigger or more beautiful than the Philippines. Decorations go up in September and stay up through January. Huge Christmas trees are everywhere. Almost everyone puts up colorful paper lanterns called *parol*. There are parades, contests for best decorations, and huge family meals.

GLOSSARY

animism (AH-nuh-miz-uhm) belief that all living things have souls or spirits

archipelago (ahr-kuh-PEL-uh-goh) group of islands

emigrated (EM-ih-grayt-id) left your home country to live in another country

Filipino (fil-uh-PEE-noh) the name of the language and the people of the Philippines

immigrants (IM-ih-gruhnts) people who have moved from one country to another and settled there

Nazarene (NAH-zuh-reen) Jesus Christ

Filipino Words

adobo (ah-DOH-boh) a stew that is the country's national dish

camaro (kah-MAH-roh) a favorite dish made out of crickets

jeepneys (JEEP-nees) jeeps that act as taxis in big cities

kamayan (kah-MAH-yan) a style of dining

Magandang araw! (mah-GAHN-dahng AH-rau) Beautiful day

Magandang gabi (mah-GAHN-dahng gah-BEE) Good night

Magandang umaga (mah-GAHN-dahng oo-MAH-gah) Good morning

parol (pah-ROHL) Christmas decorations made out of bamboo and paper

FIND OUT MORE

BOOKS

Burgan, Michael. *Philippines.* Chicago: Heinemann Library, 2012.

Jimenez, Gidget R. *All About the Philippines: Stories, Songs, Crafts, and Games for Kids.* North Clarendon, VT: Tuttle Publishing, 2015.

Olizon-Chikiamco, Norma. *Pan de Sal Saves the Day: A Filipino Children's Story.* North Clarendon, VT: Tuttle Publishing, 2009.

WEBSITES

Children International—Fast Facts about the Philippines
https://www.children.org/stories/2016/august/fast-facts-philippines
Find photographs and read facts at this website.

Easy Science for Kids—Philippines
http://easyscienceforkids.com/all-about-philippines/
See maps, videos, pictures, and more about the Philippines.

National Geographic Kids—Philippines
http://kids.nationalgeographic.com/explore/countries/
philippines/#philippines-island.jpg
Read about the country's people, geography, and language.

INDEX

ABOUT THE AUTHOR

Tamra Orr is the author of hundreds of books for readers of all ages. She graduated from Ball State University, but moved with her husband and four children to Oregon in 2001. She is a full-time author, and when she isn't researching and writing, she writes letters to friends all over the world. Orr enjoys life in the big city of Portland and feels very lucky to be surrounded by so much diversity.